KIT CARSON
in the
WEST

A Guide

Written and Illustrated by
T.H. Johnson

Published by
THE COMPUTER LAB
Box 4300
Ketchum, Idaho 83340

FAMOUS FOOTSTEPS™

guide booklets
about famous people
in their favorite places

Titles available:

Kit Carson in the West
Emily Dickinson in Amherst
Ernest Hemingway in Idaho
Ernest Hemingway in Key West
Jack London in California
Marilyn Monroe in Hollywood
Georgia O'Keeffe in New Mexico
Mark Twain in the U.S.A.
Tennessee Williams in Key West and Miami

Front cover photo: Kit Carson.
                       Courtesy of the Kit Carson Foundation
                       Taos, New Mexico.

Back cover photo: Kit Carson with a beaver hat.
                       Courtesy of the Kit Carson Memorial
                       Foundatition Inc..
                       Kit Carson Home and Museum
                       Taos, New Mexico.

ISBN 0-929-70909-8

First Edition
Copyright 1993 ⓒ The Computer Lab
printed by
Sun Litho
USA

TABLE OF CONTENTS

NOTE TO READERS

I hope readers will find this brief guide to Christopher "Kit" Carson both informative and reminiscent of bygone days when sometimes all a person had, in order to survive, were courage, intelligence and will. Times were hard but Kit loved the beauty and challenge of the untamed country. He was a mountain man, scout, military courier, farmer, Indian agent, Civil War General and Superintendent of Indian Affairs. He explored the west traveling through areas which would become the states of New Mexico, Arizona, Wyoming, Idaho, Utah, California, Washington, Oregon, Montana and Nevada.

Kit Carson was a small man but he braved the frontier as if he were a giant. By growing up in the wilderness and being a mountain man, he learned to be resourceful and how to trap, scout and communicate with the Indians. Kit became a legend in his own life time. Most who knew him respected him.

His early years were spent trapping beaver which he gave up when the market for beaver dropped. He became a hunter/trader and helped supply the frontier forts with provisions. He became a scout and guide for Fremont's expeditions. Then he was employed by the United States government as an Indian agent and finally as a volunteer during the Civil War he was enlisted to help put the Apache and Navajo Indians on reservations.

It seems as if Kit Carson's name is everywhere: forts, cities, mountains, rivers, schools, museums and even motels and restaurants are named after him. Kit Carson even appears as a character in Willa Cather's book about New Mexico, *Death Comes for the Archbishop*.

I would especially like to thank R. C. Gordon McCutchan whose help was invaluable. I would also like to extend my appreciation to Phil Petersen, Stephen Zimmer, John Colburn, Skip Miller, Scott Travis, Janice Gordon, Alejandra Aldred, Neil Poesy, Santy Rothman, Jack and Lorraine Dyson and their friend, Filbert, Joesephine Lobato, Mitch Larson, Vickie Houser, Mike Tucker, Susan Snyder, Neil Wright, Woody Bryant, Lee Bellavance, Rick Berby, Chuck Lowrie, Maragret Walsh, Joy Evens, Wayne Rickard and especially to my wife, Marsha Bellavance.

INTRODUCTION

Christopher "Kit" Carson, the sixth of ten children, was born December 24, 1809 in Madison County, Kentucky. His exploits in the west as a mountain man, scout, Indian agent and soldier would make him a legend in his lifetime. Lindsey and Rebecca Carson, Kit's parents, moved to Booneslick, Howard County, Missouri in 1811. They were settlers of the pioneer frontier. Kit's father was killed in 1818 by a falling tree. His mother remarried and at fifteen Kit was apprenticed to a saddle maker in Old Franklin, Missouri. Kit was fascinated by the stories he heard from returning mountain men who stopped by the shop for repairs.

Kit's yearning to travel west and become a trapper became too strong. In 1826 he ran away and joined a wagon train bound for Santa Fe (see page 11). He stayed in Santa Fe only a few days then traveled on to Taos (see page 29). There he spent the winter with an old friend of the Carson family, Matthew Kinkead, founder of Fort Kinkead, Missouri.

The first few years in the west were difficult for Kit. He even started back for home but changed his mind and returned. Kit had many jobs: cooking for Ewing Young, interpreting for a trading caravan and working as a teamster for a copper mine. Kit was small, liked to smoke but did not cuss or brag. He learned many languages, although he never could read or even sign his name until late in life. It is said that his Spanish was better than his English and he knew some French, ten Indian languages plus Indian sign language too.

Ewing Young then hired Kit to go on an unlicensed trapping expedition to Mexican California. Eluding the Mexican authorities the party of forty made its way to California, enduring Indian attacks and starvation before they reached the first of many missions, San Gabriel. They also stopped at other missions such as San Fernando and San Jose (See page 13).

During the years 1831 to 1840 Kit trapped for beaver in the mountain streams of Idaho, Colorado, Utah, and Wyoming. He worked the headwaters of the Snake and Salmon Rivers with Thomas

Fitzpatrick, spending several winters in Idaho. He trapped North Park in Colorado with John Gantt's fur company.

The spring of 1833 was exciting for Kit, who exhibited his extreme bravery and uncanny luck when he and five other trappers were attacked by two hundred Comanche Indians. They were vastly outnumbered and stranded in the open with no cover. Kit jumped from his mule and slit it's throat with his knife. The mule fell making a shield for Kit to hide behind. The other men followed Kit's lead. The Comanches raced in to collect scalps but were abruptly halted when their horses smelled the fresh blood. From their fortified position the trappers fired at the Indians whose bows and arrows were no match at that distance. When the Indians retreated, Kit and the others were able to escape on foot. Kit was not only brave and lucky but also cautious and resourceful.

Kit was a good hunter and was hired by several of the forts. Once Kit fired on some game only to be surprised by two large grizzly bears. Dropping his empty gun he raced toward the nearest grove of trees and climbed one. The bears, unable to climb or uproot the tree, gave up and Kit returned to camp; and from then on he was wary of grizzly bears.

In 1834 Kit attended his first mountain rendezvous on the Green River near Pinewood, Colorado. The rendezvous were started so the mountain men would not have to return to the city to sell their furs. Today people may attend rendezvous celebrations in many states (See Carson City page 23). At the 1835 rendezvous Kit won a fight he had with another trapper, the ferocious Shunar. That dispute may have been about an Arapahoe Indian woman, named Waa-nibe (Singing Grass), whom Kit later married. They lived near Fort Hall, Idaho (See page 15) and had two children, the oldest was a girl named Adaline.

When beaver prices fell the trappers were forced to find other work. Kit became a hunter for Fort Davy Crocket and then for Bent's Old Fort, Colorado (See page 17). But tragedy struck: Waa-nibe died and soon after their second child was accidently killed.

Kit decided to take Adaline east to stay with relatives and attend school. During this trip in 1842 he met Lieutenant John C. Fremont who was organizing an expedition to survey the west. This chance meeting changed his life. Because Kit knew the territory he was hired as a scout. The first expedition explored the North Platte River into western Wyoming to what is now known as Fremont Peak.

Back in Taos, Kit was baptized a Catholic and in February, 1843 he married a socially prominent New Mexican woman, Josefa Jaramillo. Although he was thirty-three and she only about fourteen, they had a happy marriage with seven children.

Fremont's second expedition in 1843 traveled to Fort Hall, Fort Boise, Fort Vancouver and Fort St. Vrain along parts of the Oregon Trail. After a historic winter crossing (see page 25) of the Sierra Nevada Mountains, Fort Sutter (see page 27) was a welcome sight when they reached it in March of 1844.

Returning home to his wife in Taos, Kit then started a ranch/farm near Cimarron but sold it at a loss when he was called upon by Fremont to join him once again.

The third expedition left from Bent's Old Fort in 1845 and headed west to the Great Salt Lake. There they explored a large island which they named Antelope Island (see page 19). They went on to cross the Great Salt Lake Desert and the Humbolt and Carson Rivers. They made it over the Sierra Nevada Mountains at Truckee Pass (Donner Summit) and on to Sutter's Fort in December 1845. By May of 1846 they were at Klamath Lake. While fighting with the Indians there, Fremont saved Kit's life. The expedition was called back to California when war broke out between the United States and Mexico. The American forces seized California and Fremont, who had been promoted to Colonel, sent Kit to Washington D.C. with dispatches.

On the way to Washington, Kit met General Kearney and his troops. The General ordered Kit to act as his guide to California, causing a conflict for Kit who felt loyal to Fremont. (Confusion over command later resulted in Fremont's court-martial.) Kearney's scout, Thomas Fitzpatrick, carried the dispatches on to Washington. During the trip Kearney ran into resistance from California immigrants who were allied with the Mexican government. Pinned down by the Californians, General Kearney was forced to send to San Diego for assistance. Two groups of couriers were sent. The first was captured but the second group, including Kit, slipped past the sentries during the night by crawling on their bellies. But they lost their shoes which they had removed to keep quiet. The thirty mile desert walk was filled with cacti and their feet were severely mutilated.

The Mexicans eventually surrendered to Fremont, who again sent Kit to Washington with dispatches. On his way Kit stopped in Taos and discovered that his wife's brother-in-law, Charles Bent, first Governor of the New Mexico Territory, had been brutally murdered by a mob of Indian and Mexican insurrectionists. Kit's wife had been staying with the Governor but escaped by digging a hole in a wall of the adobe home. Kit stayed to give testimony at the trial of the captured revolutionaries and hurried on to Washington. There he met with President Polk.

By 1849 Kit was back in Taos but was tired of running dispatches back and forth to Washington D.C., so he started a ranch/farm not too far away at Rayado (see page 31). There he was asked to help rescue a woman who had been kidnapped by the Jicarilla Apache while traveling on the Santa Fe Trail. The rescue party was headed by Major William Grier. Kit's instinct was to attack the camp at once and take the Indians by surprise but the Major ordered a halt, giving the Indians time to escape. In camp they found a dime novel about the mythical Kit Carson. Kit always regretted not being able to save the woman he felt had been relying on him. Except for Indians raiding the livestock, Rayado was uneventful. In 1852 Kit went on his last trapping trip to Colorado. In 1853 he was involved in a large sheep drive to California.

He was appointed Indian agent in March of 1854 with his office in Taos. He went on several expeditions to control hostilities between the Indians and the settlers. Since he knew the Indian ways and spoke their languages he was able to help negotiate treaties. During these years he dealt with tribes such as the Cheyenne, Navajo, Ute, Arapaho, and Apache.

During the Civil War Kit resigned as Indian agent to become Lieutenant Colonel of the New Mexico volunteers. Although his confrontations with Confederate forces were limited he impressed his commanders with his ability to carry out orders. During the Civil War the Indians returned to raiding settlements. When the war was over the United States turned it's attentions to those hostilities. Kit was ordered to mount a campaign against the Mescalero Apaches.

Kit was next sent against the great Navajo Nation located in the four corners of New Mexico, Arizona, Utah and Colorado. General Carleton ordered captured Indians sent to the Bosque Redondo at Fort Sumner in New Mexico to become farmers and ranchers. He ordered the Indians to surrender and upon receiving little response, ordered Kit to wage war on the Indians. Kit was to kill all men who could bear arms, take prisoner all women and children, appropriate all livestock and destroy all the crops. This was General Carleton's scorched earth policy. Kit had joined the military to fight Confederates not wage war on Indians, but directed by his sense of duty he followed orders. Canyon de Chelly (see page 35), the Navajo stronghold, was penetrated and cleared by Carson's troops and the long walk began for thousands of Navajos.

One Navajo's view is expressed by Tina Bighorse in her book "BIGHORSE: The Warrior", where she recounts her father's memories, "Once Kit Carson was our good friend...We never think of him as a soldier, as fighting against us, or taking us prisoners. We Navajos will never have the heart to forgive Kit Carson..."

Kit also led an expedition against the Plains Indians: Kiowas, Comanches, Apaches and Arapahoes. At the battle of Adobe Walls in the panhandle of Texas, Kit turned his withdrawal into a decisive victory which left the Plains Indians ready for peace. His success was survival: his vastly outnumbered troops had only three dead while the Indians lost over sixty.

During the Civil War Kit was promoted to Brevet Brigadier General, but afterwards was routinely reduced to Lieutenant Colonel. In 1866 he was assigned Commander of Fort Garland (see page 35).

When the New Mexico volunteers disbanded in 1867 Kit and his family moved to Boggsville, Colorado (see page 37). In 1868 he was appointed Superintendent of Indian Affairs for the Colorado Territory. Although in poor health, he made a final trip to Washington D.C. to negotiate a treaty for the Ute Indians.

Within weeks of his return home his wife died unexpectedly. A few days later Kit went to Fort Lyon for medical care and died there on May 23, 1868, at the age of fifty-eight. Kit and Josefa, were laid to rest in Taos, New Mexico (see pg. 39). Today the legacy of Kit Carson is prominent throughout the West.

Kit Carson Monument

SANTA FE

Santa Fe, New Mexico was founded in 1610 by the Spaniards and has been a seat of government longer than any other State Capital in the United States. It is located between the Pecos and Rio Grande Rivers at the base of the Sangre De Cristo Mountains. The oldest road in the United States, El Camino Real, was the supply route from Chihuahua, Mexico to Santa Fe. When trade started between Mexico and the United States in the 1830's the Santa Fe Trail was the link to Saint Louis and the eastern United States.

The architecture of Santa Fe is very distinctive: adobe walls, flat roofs made of earth, and ceilings herringboned with latias. The two styles of architecture are the territorial and pueblo. The Palace of the Governors was built in 1610 and is an example of territorial style. The central plaza across the street from the Palace is a gathering place for the community.

Kit arrived in 1826 from Missouri but did not stay long in Santa Fe, traveling on to Taos. Most trappers preferred to live in Taos because there was less government scrutiny. Jobs were scarce and Kit worked as a cook, an interpreter and a teamster. In 1829 Kit hired on with Ewing Young for a California trapping expedition leaving from Santa Fe. During the years of the Navajo campaign Kit corresponded with the military headquarters located in Santa Fe.

Today a statue commemorating Kit stands in front of the Federal Building, north of the Plaza at the intersection of Lincoln Street and Federal Place. Evergreen trees tower over the statue giving shade to the nearby benches. The statue was erected by the Masonic Lodge and is inscribed "He led the way". Kit joined the Montezuma Lodge of the Masons in Santa Fe in 1854. The Bent Lodge in Taos owns the Kit Carson Home/Museum there (see page 29).

The Palace of the Governors, now a museum, is on Palace Avenue and contains artifacts of the Carson days. An Indian street market is set up daily along the avenue. The Plaza is surrounded by a mecca of stores and shops promoting the southwest style. For more information contact the Santa Fe Convention and Visitor's Bureau at (800) 777-2489.

THJ
© 1990

Mission San Jose

MISSION SAN JOSE

Mission San Jose was founded in 1797 by Father Fermin Francisco de Lasuen, a Franciscan padre. It was the fourteenth of twenty-one missions to be built in California. The beautiful white adobe structure with red tile roof is off Interstate 680 at the intersection of Washington and Mission in Fremont, California. Largely destroyed by an earthquake in 1868, the remaining original portion now houses a museum and gift shop. The chapel, which had been built in 1809, has been authentically reconstructed.

Kit first came to California on an unlicensed trapping expedition with Ewing Young in 1830. They trapped as far north as the Sacramento River. On their return they were approached by the alcade and fifteen other Indians of the San Jose Mission to help return a few runaway Indians. Young, hoping to gain favor with the Padre of the prosperous mission, volunteered the help of eleven men, led by Kit. A fight with an unfriendly Indian village lasted all day but with the danger that all would be killed, the hostile village returned the runaways. During their stay at the mission Ewing Young also sold furs to a ship then anchored in the port.

Among the missions Kit visited were San Fernando, San Gabriel and San Jose. Sometimes they traveled on the "El Camino Real" as the royal roads were called. The missions gradually began to decline after Mexico gained its independence from Spain and financial ties were severed.

Years later, John Fremont, for whom Fremont, California is named, surveyed and explored the west with Kit scouting the way. Both the 1843-44 and 1845-46 expeditions came through California. Fremont wrote about Kit in his daily journals and these tales of his exploits made Kit famous. The expedition of 1845-46 was involved in the fight for California's independence from Mexico. Their adventures took them all over California from Sacramento, Sutter's Fort, and Monterey, to San Diego and Los Angeles.

The museum and gift shop at the mission are open seven days a week, from 10am to 5pm. A video about the mission is also available. Call (510) 657-1797 for additional information.

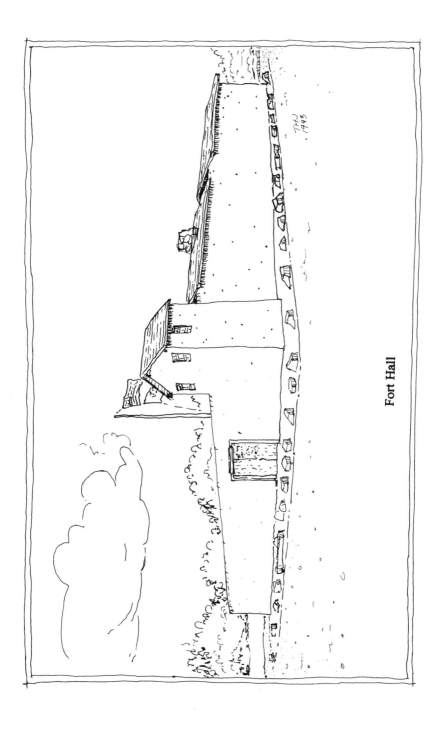

Fort Hall

FORT HALL

The original Fort Hall was built by Nathaniel Wyeth in 1834. It was located on the Snake River in southeast Idaho in an area called "The Bottoms", a favorite hunting ground of the Shoshone-Bannock Indians. Today that site is on the nearby Fort Hall Indian Reservation and not open to the public. The original fort has long since vanished, but there is a replica in Upper Ross Park, Pocatello, Idaho. The entry is on the 2900 Block of South 4th Avenue.

Built of adobe bricks the fort offered the mountain men a safe haven to rest, trade and sell furs. Fort Hall was named after Henry Hall of Boston, one of Wyeth's financial backer's. Under strong competition from the Hudson Bay Company's Fort Boise, Wyeth sold out to them in 1837. They operated the fort until it was sold to the United States in 1855. The fort was the gateway to the Oregon territory and also a crossroad to the Great Salt Lake. Tracks from the Oregon Trail, which celebrated its 150th anniversary in 1993, are still visible in some areas.

Kit trapped beaver and hunted buffalo for the fort in 1836. Today only a few captive buffalo graze nearby but there were once large herds in the area. Entries in a Hudson Bay Company accounting ledger show that Kit traded with the fort during the summer of 1837. That part of the ledger is on display at the fort in Pocatello. Since Kit bought beads, it is supposed that they were for his wife, Waa-nibe.

Kit was also at Fort Hall during his travels with Fremont. On the second expedition in 1843, Fremont went ahead to the Salt Lake while Kit detoured to Fort Hall for supplies. Although Kit was able to get some provisions, the stocks at the fort had been depleted by emigrants.

Building the fort replica was a project of the 1963 Bannock County Centennial Committee. It is open from April to October and daily from 9 am to 7 pm, Memorial Day thru Labor Day. A history display and video are also available. For more information call (208) 234-6233 or 234-1795. The adjacent Bannock County Historical Museum contains local artifacts. Both fort and museum are in Ross Park which also has playgrounds, picnic tables and even a zoo.

Kit Carson At Bent's Fort
Courtesy of the Kit Carson Museum

BENT'S OLD FORT

Bent's Old Fort was built on the Arkansas River in 1833. It is off State Highway 194 in southeastern Colorado, seven miles east of La Junta. It was owned by the partnership of Charles Bent, William Bent and Ceran St. Vrain. It was built to capitalize on trade with the Plains Indians and the caravans on the mountain route of the Santa Fe Trail. The deteriorated fort was reconstructed by the National Park Service in 1976.

William Bent, known as "Little White Man" by the Indians, supervised the construction. Made from local materials, the large adobe structure was also known as Fort William. A double gateway opened onto a plaza surrounded by workshops, workers quarters, store rooms, kitchen, dining room and even a billiard room. There was a large press for baling beaver skins and buffalo hides. There were towers at opposite corners and a corral at the perimeter. Residents included a carpenter, blacksmith, gunsmith, wheelwright and tailor. Interior rooms had dirt floors, adobe walls and ceilings of latias. Water was drawn from a well inside the fort. For weary travelers it offered the best accommodations between St. Louis and Santa Fe.

The rumor that Kit helped build the fort is not true. At the time he was trapping with Captain Gantt in South Park, Colorado. He did, however, spend eight months as a hunter for the fort in 1841. Kit joined Fremont's third expedition at the fort in 1845.

William Bent abandoned the fort in 1849 after Ceran St. Vrain failed to sell it to the U.S. government. The often reported story that Bent burned his fort is now considered unlikely by historians. Later the fort was considered a good overnight stop on the Santa Fe Trail and Kit stayed here in 1851. It was a U.S. Postal Stage Station from 1861 to 1873.

Today the fort is a National Historic Site and is open from 8 am to 4:30 pm (until 6 pm in the summer). Thanksgiving, Christmas and New Year are the only days it closes! There is a small admission fee. A twenty minute video tape about the fort is available on request. There is a giftshop and restroom but no food or snack bar. For more information call (719) 384-2596.

Kit's Cross On Fremont Island

ANTELOPE ISLAND

Antelope Island is located at the south end of the Great Salt Lake in Utah. A causeway, more than seven miles long, connects the island to the mainland at Syracuse just south of Ogden. It's just a few minutes from Interstate 15. The 28,000 acre island juts into the lake and is clearly visible from Salt Lake City.

There is a smaller island to the north of Antelope Island which Kit helped explore during the second Fremont expedition in 1843. They made the fifteen mile trip in an experimental rubber boat which they had trouble keeping inflated. The island was barren and desolate, void of any animal life with no fresh water so they called it Disappointment Island. While there Kit chiseled a cross into a rock outcropping at the summit and Fremont lost a lens cap cover. On the way to the mainland they were caught in a storm and had to work to keep the boat afloat. These type of experiences caused Kit to dislike travel by water. The island was renamed Fremont island in 1849 by Captain Stansbury. It is privately owned and not open to the public.

The third Fremont expedition in 1845 explored Antelope Island, named after the antelope that inhabited it. Low water enabled them to reach the island on horseback. They stayed for several days making observations and eating the plentiful game. Back on shore an Indian demanded, and received, payment for the antelope they had eaten! After about two weeks surveying the lake they headed west across the Great Salt Lake Desert looking for a route to California. Kit and three others scouted ahead in search of grass and water, which they found near what is now called Pilot Peak in Nevada.

Antelope Island, now a State Park, has a herd of six hundred buffalo. The last of the original antelope died in 1933 but they were re-introduced in 1993. The park is also home to deer. wildcats, coyotes and numerous waterfowl. Antelope Island has two beaches, picnic and shower facilities as well as a marina on the north end. There are plans for a Visitor's Center with interpretive exhibits and a historical video. Restrooms are also available. If you have questions call (801) 451-3397.

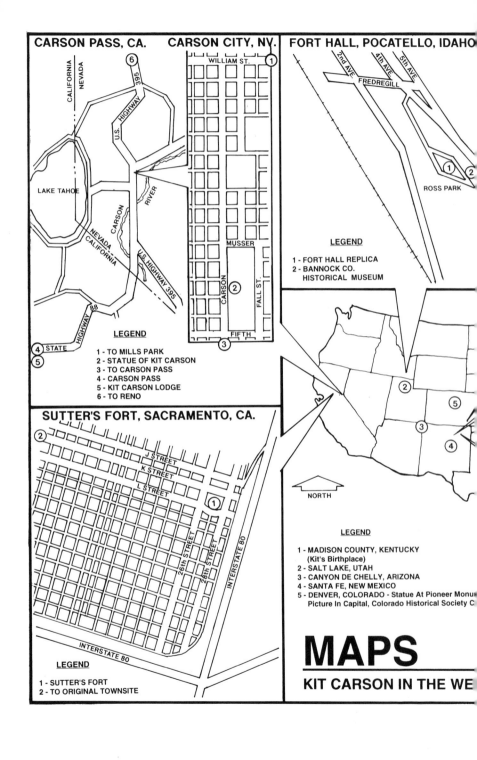

CARSON PASS, CA.

LEGEND
1 - TO MILLS PARK
2 - STATUE OF KIT CARSON
3 - TO CARSON PASS
4 - CARSON PASS
5 - KIT CARSON LODGE
6 - TO RENO

CARSON CITY, NV.

WILLIAM ST.
MUSSER
FIFTH

FORT HALL, POCATELLO, IDAHO

2nd AVE
4th AVE
5th AVE
FREDREGILL
ROSS PARK

LEGEND
1 - FORT HALL REPLICA
2 - BANNOCK CO.
HISTORICAL MUSEUM

NORTH

LEGEND
1 - MADISON COUNTY, KENTUCKY
(Kit's Birthplace)
2 - SALT LAKE, UTAH
3 - CANYON DE CHELLY, ARIZONA
4 - SANTA FE, NEW MEXICO
5 - DENVER, COLORADO - Statue At Pioneer Monu
Picture In Capital, Colorado Historical Society C

SUTTER'S FORT, SACRAMENTO, CA.

J STREET
K STREET
L STREET
26th STREET
28th STREET
INTERSTATE 80
INTERSTATE 80

LEGEND
1 - SUTTER'S FORT
2 - TO ORIGINAL TOWNSITE

MAPS

KIT CARSON IN THE WE

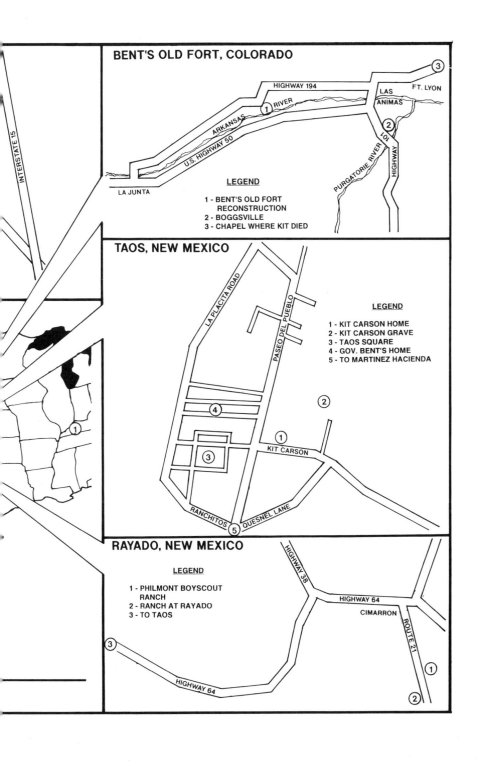

BENT'S OLD FORT, COLORADO

HIGHWAY 194
FT. LYON
LAS ANIMAS
ARKANSAS RIVER
U.S. HIGHWAY 50
INTERSTATE 15
PURGATORIE RIVER
HIGHWAY 101
LA JUNTA

LEGEND

1 - BENT'S OLD FORT
    RECONSTRUCTION
2 - BOGGSVILLE
3 - CHAPEL WHERE KIT DIED

TAOS, NEW MEXICO

LA PLACITA ROAD
PASEO DEL PUEBLO
KIT CARSON
RANCHITOS
QUESNEL LANE

LEGEND

1 - KIT CARSON HOME
2 - KIT CARSON GRAVE
3 - TAOS SQUARE
4 - GOV. BENT'S HOME
5 - TO MARTINEZ HACIENDA

RAYADO, NEW MEXICO

HIGHWAY 38
HIGHWAY 64
CIMARRON
ROUTE 21
HIGHWAY 64

LEGEND

1 - PHILMONT BOYSCOUT
    RANCH
2 - RANCH AT RAYADO
3 - TO TAOS

Carson Pass Information Station/Museum

CARSON CITY

Carson City, the capital of Nevada, was named in 1858 after the Carson River which runs nearby. Colonel John C. Fremont had named the river after his scout, Kit Carson. The groves of cottonwood trees which grow along the river bank provide shade and shelter and were favorite campsites of the Fremont expeditions. Nearby Carson Lake, Carson Sink and Carson Pass (See page 25) also commemorate Kit.

Fremont hired Kit as a scout for his western expeditions. The expedition of 1843-44 searched for the mythical Buenaventura River and explored the Great Basin along the Sierra Nevada Mountains. The Washo Indians who lived along the Carson River told of a white settlement across the mountains and helped direct the expedition. The Indians also warned of the deep snow saying it would be impossible to cross the mountains so late in the year (see Carson Pass page 25). The Expedition of 1845-46 explored the Great Basin and mapped a route to California.

Kit returned to this area in 1853 when he drove a flock of sheep he had purchased cheaply in New Mexico to the California gold fields, making a big profit. Carson City grew mainly due to the discovery of silver. (The nearby mining boom town of Virginia City is also a popular tourist attraction.)

A statue of Kit Carson on horseback, scouting the way, is located on the Legislative Mall on Carson Street in Carson City. The artist, Buckeye Blake, was commissioned by the famed Ormsby House Hotel and Casino to create the bronze statue. There was a dedication ceremony on June 10, 1989 during the Kit Carson Rendezvous. A plaque mounted below the statue has a map showing the routes of the trips which Kit made through Nevada.

The Kit Carson Rendezvous and Wagon Train Days celebration is held each year at Mills Park, usually on the second weekend in June. Admission is free. Events include dancing, cowboy and western music, a barbecue, horseshoe contest and an exhibit of authentic western crafts. Visitors can see the skills and dress of the mountain men. A wagon train even travels from Reno to Carson City. For more information call 800-NEVADA-1.

Kit Carson Rendezvous Days

CARSON PASS

Carson Pass, named after Kit Carson, is in the Sierra Nevada Mountains at an elevation of 8650 feet. The Pass is about 35 miles south of Tahoe on California State Highway 88 and is open year-round.

Fremont's historic 1843-44 winter crossing of these mountains was accomplished through the sheer determination of Fremont and his men. The snow had to be beaten down with mallets so the horses could pass and some of their equipment had to be abandoned. With Kit leading the way they reached the summit on February 6, 1844. Kit recognized the Sacramento Valley he had trapped with Ewing Young fourteen years before. Four weeks later they reached Sutter's Fort (see page 27). Fremont's third expedition passed through the mountains farther north near Truckee.

In 1853 Kit helped organize a drive of 6500 sheep from New Mexico to California. They used the Emigrant Trail through Carson Pass and sold the sheep at a profit in Sacramento.

The Carson Pass Information Station/Museum, at the summit, has a museum depicting Fremont's winter crossing and the Emigrant Trail story. The station is open from June to mid-September. Carson's name was once carved on a tree at the summit (who carved it is uncertain) and a monument commemorating the "Carson tree" is nearby. Many hikes originate here, at the principal Mokelumne Wilderness trailhead. About a half mile east of the station, the Red Lake Vista turnout also has a historical plaque about Carson.

Just below the summit, camping, lodging, gas, boat rentals and food are available at the Caples Lake Resort (209) 258-8888. Horseback riding, mountain biking, hiking and skiing are available in the Kirkwood area and meals can be had at the historic Kirkwood Inn. Summer facilities are available at the Kit Carson Lodge (209) 258-8500 on Silver Lake. There are boat rentals, swimming, a restaurant, store, post office, laundromat and rental cabins. Kay's Silver Lake Resort (209) 258-8598 has a store, coffee shop, gas and marina too. The El Dorado National Forest (209) 295-4251 also maintains a picnic area and campground at Silver Lake.

Sutter's Fort

THJ
© 1990

SUTTER'S FORT

In 1839 Captain John August Sutter received a 45,000 acre Mexican Land Grant in trade for building a fort. Sutter built his white adobe fort near the confluence of the Sacramento and America Rivers in the Sacramento Valley. He called his new settlement "New Helvetia" (New Switzerland). Today the fort is surrounded by the city, on L Street between 26th and 28th Street adjacent to the State Indian Museum in Sacramento, California.

Kit Carson's first visit to the Sacramento Valley was with Ewing Young. It was Kit's first trapping expedition and the furthest West he had ever been. He spent that summer of 1830 hunting in the Sacramento Valley.

Kit returned to the Sacramento Valley in 1844 with Fremont. That expedition made the first winter crossing of the Sierra Nevada Mountains. They stayed at Sutter's Fort for only a few days to recoup and get needed supplies from Captain Sutter, who was a gracious host.

Fremont's third expedition brought Kit to the valley again in 1845. That expedition was entangled in California's fight for independence from Mexico. Colonel Fremont supported the July, 1846 Bear Flag Revolt at Sonoma and the raising of the American flag over Sutter's Fort. Since Sutter was a Mexican citizen, Fremont changed the fort's name to Fort Sacramento. Some of these actions would later lead to Fremont's court martial.

Everything changed for Sutter and his fort when James Marshall found gold on the American River. News of the discovery caused the gold rush of 1849. Soon gold fever stole Sutter's workers and destroyed his business. In 1853 Carson drove 6500 sheep from New Mexico to Sacramento to help supply the demand for food created by this influx.

Today Sutter's Fort Historic Park is a part of the California State Park System. There is a small admission fee. Self guided tours with multi-lingual audio wands are available. No food is allowed inside but picnic tables are provided outside. The Fort is open daily except Thanksgiving, Christmas and New Year's Day from 10 a.m, to 5 p.m. For more information about special events such as Living History Days, call 1 (916) 445-4422.

Kit Carson Home And Museum

TAOS HOME

The Kit Carson Home and Museum is located a half block east of the Taos Plaza on Kit Carson Road in Taos, New Mexico. Although Kit traveled to many places, he established roots in Taos at an early age and always considered it his home. At an elevation of 6950 feet Taos is surrounded by the Carson National Forest.

Kit was sixteen when he first came to Taos in 1826, eager to become a mountain man. Although he was small, he was hired for a trapping expedition to California led by Ewing Young.

In 1843 Kit married Josefa Jaramillo, daughter of a prominent Taos family. The wedding was conducted by Padre Martinez at the Guadalupe Catholic Church. (The Martinez Hacienda in Taos is now a museum.) Kit's U shaped adobe home was a wedding present to his wife.

Kit's house was originally built in 1825 and had a flat roof and twelve rooms. It was here they raised seven children of their own, some children of Charles Bent's and a few Indian children too.

During the Taos Rebellion of 1847 Josefa was staying with her brother-in-law, Governor Charles Bent and his family. (His nearby home is also open to the public.) An angry mob came to the Governor's house and brutally assassinated him. The family narrowly escaped through a hole they had dug in the back wall of the adobe house. Kit was in California and did not learn of the rebellion until he was sent as a courier to Washington D. C. He stopped in Taos in April of 1847 but stayed only briefly before going on to Washington. In 1849 Fremont was on his return from a disastrous expedition when he stopped to visit Kit in Taos. Kit was Indian Agent in Taos from 1854 until 1861. He would sit outside, smoking his pipe and conferring with the Indians.

When Kit and Josefa died, the house was sold to support the children. In 1952 the house was renovated by the Bent Masonic Lodge. It is now operated by the Kit Carson Historic Museums. It has a large display of Carson artifacts that tell the story of his life. Three of the eight rooms are furnished as they might have been when the Carson family lived there. It is open daily: summer 8 am to 6 pm, winter 9 am to 5 pm. For more information call (505)-758-0505.

Ranch At Rayado

RANCH AT RAYADO

Kit's home at Rayado is on Route 21, eleven miles south of Cimarron on the Philmont Scout Ranch in northeastern New Mexico. Little was left of the original building. In 1950 it was reconstructed to what is thought might have existed when Kit lived there and today it is called the Kit Carson Museum.

When Mexico gained independence from Spain in 1821, trade increased between the States and Santa Fe. The Santa Fe Trail's mountain branch passed through Cimarron and the ruts left by the wagon wheels can still be seen. A stone marker near the Kit Carson Museum commemorates the Santa Fe Trail and was placed there by The Daughters of the American Revolution and the Territory of New Mexico.

Kit first lived in the area when he was farming near the Little Cimarron in 1845. He and Richard Owens planted grain but when they found out that Fremont was in the territory preparing for his third expedition, they sold the farm and went to join him.

Kit returned to this area in 1849 when he joined Lucien Maxwell in a business enterprise at Rayado. Maxwell owned an immense tract of land and his home, next to the Carson Museum, is a registered cultural property. On one venture Kit went with a trade wagon train back to St. Louis. Kit built a home in Rayado but did not move his family to it until 1851. Kit's daughter, Adaline, lived here until she married and moved to California. While at Rayado, Kit was enlisted by the military to help rescue a Mrs. White who had been captured by some Indians. They were unable to save her and Kit always felt bad about that failure.

The Kit Carson Museum is open daily: 8am to 5pm Memorial Day to Labor Day. It is operated by the Boy Scouts, who dress in period costumes and give free tours and demonstrations. No food or restrooms available. The Philmont Museum, about seven miles from the Carson Museum, contains art and history of the area. It is open Monday to Friday from 8 am to 5 pm, free, restrooms available. Call (505) 376-2281 for more information. In nearby Cimarron, there is the interesting Old Mill Museum, as well as food and lodging at The Kit Carson Inn and the historic St. James Hotel.

Visitor's Center At Canyon de Chelly

CANYON DE CHELLY

Canyon de Chelly, now a National Monument, was the strong-hold of the Navajo Indians. It is located in the Northeast corner of Arizona on the Navajo Indian Reservation near the town of Chinle, Arizona on Highways 64 and 191.

The beautiful sandstone canyon has been inhabited for centuries by Indian tribes including Anasazi, Pueblo and Navajo. Cliff dwellings, hogans, pictographs and petroglyphs are a common sight.

Before 1863 the Navajos frequently raided Spanish and Pueblo settlements for livestock, supplies and women. In 1863 the United States decided to end these hostilities. General Carleton ordered his troops to make war on the Navajos with his "scorched earth policy". Colonel Kit Carson was assigned this duty. Although he did not want to fight the Navajo, he felt obligated by both loyalty and his oath. Carson's troops were the first non-Indians to fully explore and traverse the entire canyon. During a nine month campaign of destruction in the canyon about nine thousand Indians surrendered or were captured. They were sent to Fort Sumner at Bosque Redondo in east central New Mexico. Their journey is known as the "Long Walk". Four years later the relocation proved to be a failure and the Navajos were allowed to return to their home.

Today Canyon de Chelly is a popular tourist attraction, although some Navajo still live there growing crops and herding sheep. Accommodations at the canyon are available at the Thunderbird Lodge. A cafeteria and gift shop provide tourists amenities. Food and accommodations are also available in nearby Chinle. To view the canyon as Kit did, one can rent horses and take a ride into the canyon. For those on foot the short three mile hike to White House Ruin is the only access into the canyon that does not require a guide. The Visitor Center is open daily and contains an excellent small museum depicting the canyon's history, a gift shop and Navajo hogan. A movie about Canyon de Chelly is available, check with the Visitor Center for showing times. If you have further questions call the Information Center at (602) 674-5500.

Commandant's Quarters At Fort Garland

FORT GARLAND

Fort Garland was built in 1858 in what is now Southern Colorado. It is twenty-five miles east of Alamosa off U.S. 160 and also on the Old Kit Carson Trail, now Colorado Route 159. It is only seventy-six miles north of Taos. The fort consists of a quadrangle of low flat roofed adobe buildings which have changed little over the years. It's purpose was to protect the settlers of the San Luis Valley.

Kit took command of Fort Garland and its sixty-five New Mexico volunteers in 1866. His rank had been reduced from Brevet Brigadier General to Lieutenant Colonel as was the normal policy after the Civil War.

An increase in the number of settlers put pressure on the local resources and caused tension with the Ute Indians. Kit's job was to keep the peace. During his life Kit had many hostile encounters with Indians but was considered an Indian-lover by some because he only killed Indians who deserved punishment. He could speak and communicate with them and he understood their problems and needs. When notorious Civil War General Sherman visited the fort he observed that, "These Redskins think Kit twice as big as me....and they would believe him and trust him any day before me". General Rusling noted: "Kit returned this confidence, by being their most steadfast and unswerving friend. He declared all our Indian troubles were caused originally by bad white men...".

Kit was at the fort for only one year. When the New Mexico Volunteers were disbanded, he was mustered out of the service. While at Fort Garland he had experienced chest pains and a bad cough and could no longer ride horseback. In the summer of 1867 he moved with his family to Boggsville (see page 37).

Fort Garland was abandoned in 1883 and is now maintained by the Colorado Historical Society. The Commandant's Quarters have been restored to the days of Carson's command. Replicas of Kit and his wife Josefa are on display. From April 1 until October 31, the fort is open daily from 9 am to 5 pm. During the rest of the year it is open from 8 am to 4 pm but closed on Tuesdays and Wednesdays. A small admission fee is required. For more information call (719)-379-3512.

Kit Carson Chapel, Fort Lyon, Colorado

BOGGSVILLE

After leaving Fort Garland in 1867, Kit and his family moved to Boggsville, Colorado. It is two miles south of Las Animas on Highway 101, about 13 miles from Bent's Fort. The family lived in a six room house which Thomas Boggs had built next to the Purgatoire River.

Shortly after they moved to Boggsville Kit was appointed Superintendent of Indian Affairs for the Colorado Territory. He was requested to travel to Washington D.C. and give testimony concerning the treaty with the Ute Indians. Although his health was poor he considered it his duty to do his best for the Ute chiefs. While in the east he consulted doctors regarding his chest pains. Dr. Tilton, assistant surgeon at Fort Lyon, had earlier diagnosed his pains as being caused by an aneurysm of the aorta. There was little that could be done.

Kit returned home by train to Cheyenne, Wyoming where he caught the stage to Denver. His health was so poor he had to stay and recoup at the Planter's House. Shortly after Kit returned to Boggsville, Josefa died unexpectedly from complications of childbirth. This was a shock for Kit, who continued to deteriorate. He was moved to Dr. Tilton's home at Fort Lyon. For his last dinner he had a buffalo steak and smoke from his pipe. Kit died at Fort Lyon on May 23, 1868. He was buried with military honors next to Josefa in Boggsville. The bodies were later moved to Rayado and finally to Taos (see page 39). Some of Kit's children remained and were raised by the Boggs family.

The Doctor's residence where Kit died is on the grounds of the Veterans Hospital at Fort Lyon and not a tourist site. The roof was changed when it was turned into a chapel. Today it is called the "Kit Carson Chapel" and a picture of Kit hangs in the entry. Fort Lyon is on Highway 50.

The history of Boggsville is told at information stations along a path through what was the town, which is now being reconstructed. Kit's last home and barn were washed away by the flooding Purgatoire River. Picnic tables are available. The Boggsville Revitalization Committee manages the site, call (719) 456-0822. In nearby Las Animas there is gas, food and a pioneer museum named after Kit Carson.

Gravesite At Taos, New Mexico

KIT CARSON'S GRAVE

Kit Carson is buried in the Kit Carson Cemetery which is in the Kit Carson Memorial Park. The Park is located on the Paseo Del Pueblo Norte and Armory Street not far from Kit's home and the Taos Plaza. A plaque which gives a brief history of Kit Carson is just in front of a low wrought iron fence which surrounds the Carson family plot.

When Kit died at Fort Lyon he was buried next to his wife Josefa in Boggsville (see page 37). According to Kit's wishes, set forth in a letter to Aloys Scheurich, their bodies were to be buried in Taos with no church service. One year after they had been buried in Boggsville their bodies were exhumed and reburied in Taos, New Mexico.

Shortly before dying, while at Fort Lyon, Kit had made a will providing that all his assets be used for the care of his children and naming Thomas Boggs as executor of the estate, which amounted to about nine thousand dollars.

Today the United States flag flies twenty-four hours a day at both the Taos Plaza and Kit's grave. This is to commemorate an event during the Civil War when the flag was threatened by Confederate sympathizers in the Taos Plaza. Kit and others defended the American flag in the Plaza, guarding it night and day to show their support for the Union. Today Kit is honored for that act with a flag flying at his grave day and night!

In 1908 the masons of Taos erected a marble headstone for Kit's grave; his sons, Kit Jr. and Charles erected one for Josefa. Kit and Josefa's youngest daughter, Josefita Squire, was recently re-interred alongside them, causing a controversy because other bones were disturbed in the process.

The Kit Carson Cemetery and the Kit Carson Memorial Park are open everyday of the year from dawn to dusk. The cemetery has several other notable residents, such as Padre Martinez. The park has many recreational facilities plus restrooms, drinking fountain, a stage, barbecues and picnic tables.

BIBLIOGRAPHY

Bighorse, Tiana, *BIGHORSE THE WARRIOR*. Tucson, Arizona: The University of Arizona Press, 1990.

Blackwelder, Bernice. *GREAT WESTERNER The Story of Kit Carson*. Caldwell, Idaho: The Cazton Printers Ltd. 1962.

Burdett, Charles. *THE LIFE OF KIT CARSON The Great Western Hunter and Guide*. New York & Chicago: A.L. Burt Co., 1902.

Carter, Harvey Lewis. *"Dear Old Kit" The Historical Christopher Carson*. Norman & London: University of Oklahoma Press, 1968.

Egan, Ferol. *"Fremont" Explorer for a Restless Nation*. Reno, Neveda: University of Neveda Press, 1985.

Estergreen, M. Morgan. *KIT CARSON A Portrait in Courage*. Norman: University of Oklahoma Press, 1982.

Grant, Blanche C. *Kit Carson's Own Story of His Life*. Taos, New Mexico: Kit Carson Memorial Foundation In., 1955.

Guild, Thelma S. & Harvey L. Carter. *Kit Carson A pattern for Heroes*. Lincoln & London: University of Nebraska Press, 1984.

Kelley, Lawrence C. *NAVAJO Roundup*. Boulder, Colorado: The Pruett Publishing Company, 1970

Lavender, David. *BENT'S FORT*. Lincoln/London: University of Nebraska Press, 1954.

Quaife, Milo Milton. *Kit Carson's Autobiography*. Lincoln & London: University of Nebraska Press, 1966.

Robertson, Frank C. *FORT HALL Gateway to the Oregon Country*. New York: Hastings House Publishers, 1963.

Trafzer, Clifford E. *THE KIT CARSON CAMPAIGN The Last Great Navajo War*. Norman: University of Oklahoma Press, 1983.

Vestal, Stanley. *KIT CARSON The Happy Warrior of the Old West*. Boston & New York: Houghton Mifflin Co., 1928.